# Panda Planet

# DEDICATION

For Mama Bear
from Bratty Bear

*Thanks for making me feel safe to climb!*

EcoMavenLabs

www.ecomavenlabs.com

# Table of Contents

# The Giant Panda

# Introducing the
# Panda Family

Welcome to "Panda Planet", a fascinating adventure into the world of pandas! Pandas are incredible creatures with their iconic black and white coat patterns that make them instantly recognizable. But did you know that there are different species of pandas facing challenges in their natural habitats?

The giant panda, known for its cuddly appearance, is found in China and faces threats from habitat loss and low birth rates. The red panda, a smaller cousin of the giant panda, is also at risk from deforestation, illegal trade, and climate change in Asia. And let's not forget the adorable sun bear, also known as the honey bear, found in Southeast Asia, which is threatened by deforestation, poaching, and habitat fragmentation.

But there's hope! Conservation efforts are underway to protect these lovable pandas and their habitats. Scientists are researching, organizations are educating, and habitats are being preserved. With increased awareness, support, and action, we can help secure a brighter future for pandas and ensure that these playful creatures continue to thrive in the wild.

Join us on this exciting journey as we explore the world of pandas, learn about their different species, and discover how we can all play a role in protecting these amazing animals. Get ready for a fun-filled adventure of discovery and conservation with "Panda Planet"!

# Dwarf Panda

# The Diverse Panda Species

Pandas are amazing bears with different species found in different parts of the world. Let's explore their differences!

**Giant Panda (Ailuropoda melanoleuca)** - These cuddly creatures are native to China's dense bamboo forests, where they dine almost exclusively on bamboo. They are solitary animals, spending most of their time eating and resting. However, their habitat is shrinking due to deforestation and climate change, making them vulnerable to extinction.

**Red Panda (Ailurus fulgens)** - These adorable pandas are found in the high mountains of Nepal, India, Bhutan, and China. They have a diverse diet that includes bamboo, fruits, and insects. Red pandas are skilled tree climbers and are known for their playful and social behavior. However, they face habitat loss due to deforestation and climate change, making them endangered.

**Qinling Panda (Ailuropoda melanoleuca qinlingensis)** - This subspecies of the Giant Panda is found only in the Qinling Mountains of China. They have a diet similar to the Giant Panda and share the same threats of habitat loss and climate change.

**Ailuropoda microta** - This recently discovered panda species, also known as the Miniature Panda or the Dwarf Panda, is found in the high mountains of Myanmar. They have a diet that includes bamboo, fruits, and insects, and are currently facing threats from habitat loss and climate change.

It is essential that we take action to mitigate the impacts of climate change to ensure the survival of these precious pandas for future generations to enjoy.

# Red Panda

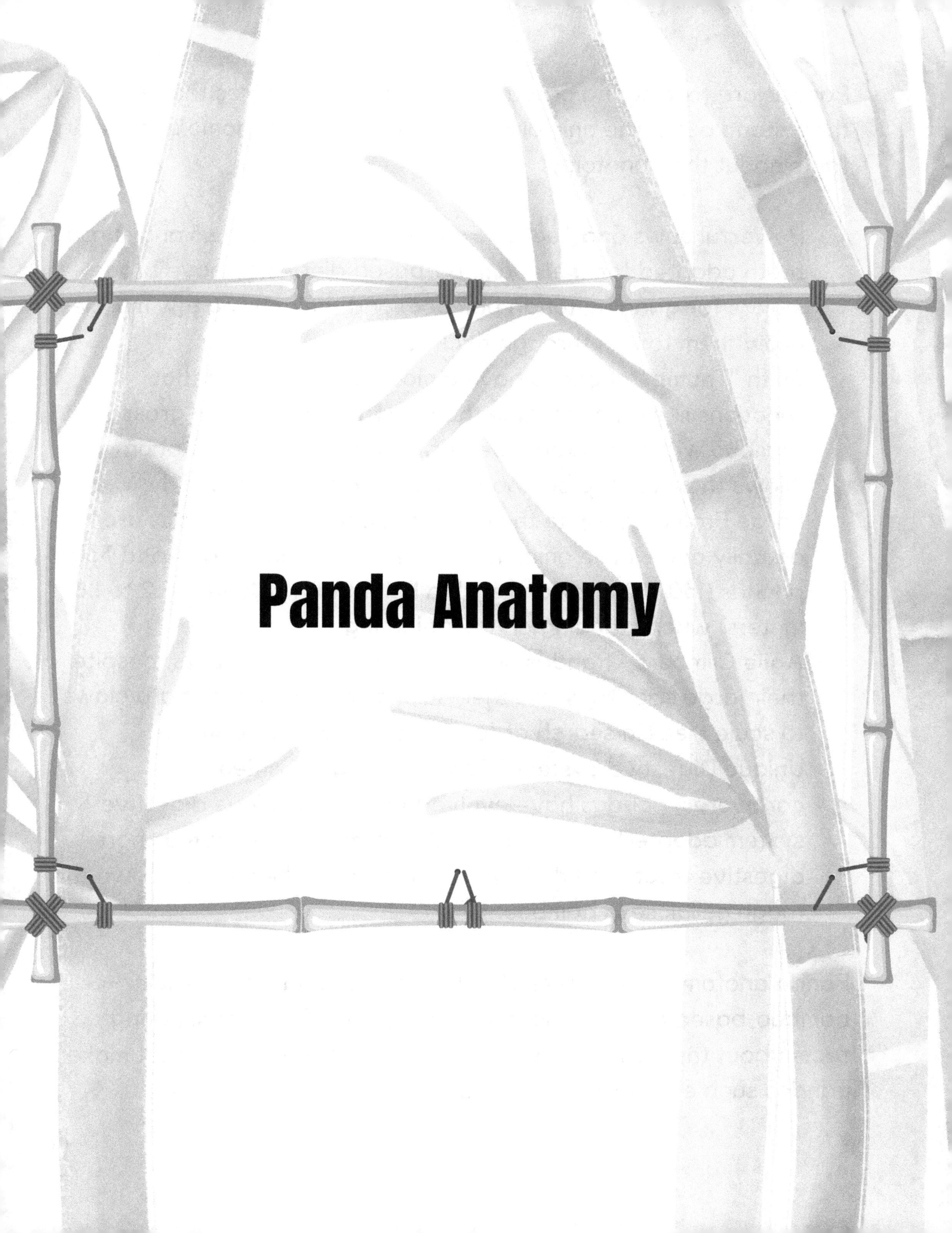

# Panda Anatomy

Pandas are fascinating creatures with unique features that make them stand out in the animal kingdom. Let's explore some interesting facts about their anatomy!

- Powerful Jaws and Teeth - Pandas have strong jaws and sharp teeth adapted for their bamboo-based diet. They have broad molars for grinding tough bamboo, and their strong jaw muscles allow them to bite through thick stalks.
- Sixth "Thumb" - Pandas have a modified wrist bone that functions like an opposable thumb, which helps them grasp bamboo with remarkable dexterity. This unique adaptation allows them to strip bamboo leaves and stems efficiently.
- Large Frame - Despite their cuddly appearance, pandas are actually quite large animals. Adult pandas can weigh up to 330 pounds (150 kg) and can reach a height of 4 to 6 feet (1.2 to 1.8 meters) when standing on their hind legs.
- Agile Climbers - Pandas are surprisingly agile climbers, despite their large size. They use their strong forelimbs and sharp claws to scale trees in search of food or to escape predators.
- Unique Digestive System - Despite being classified as carnivores, pandas have evolved to have a unique digestive system adapted for a bamboo-based diet. They have a short digestive tract, and their gut bacteria help them break down the tough cellulose in bamboo.

Panda anatomy is truly remarkable and well-adapted to their bamboo-based diet and mountainous habitat. These fascinating facts about their anatomy showcase the unique features that make pandas such extraordinary animals.

One of the unique features of pandas is their wrist bone that acts like a thumb. This specialized adaptation allows pandas to have a remarkable grasping ability, enabling them to hold and manipulate bamboo with ease. The panda's "thumb" is actually an elongated wrist bone that has evolved to be an essential tool for their herbivorous diet. This adaptation allows pandas to strip leaves from bamboo stems, peel off tough layers, and hold onto bamboo stalks while eating, showcasing their remarkable adaptability to their bamboo-rich habitat.

# Panda Skeleton

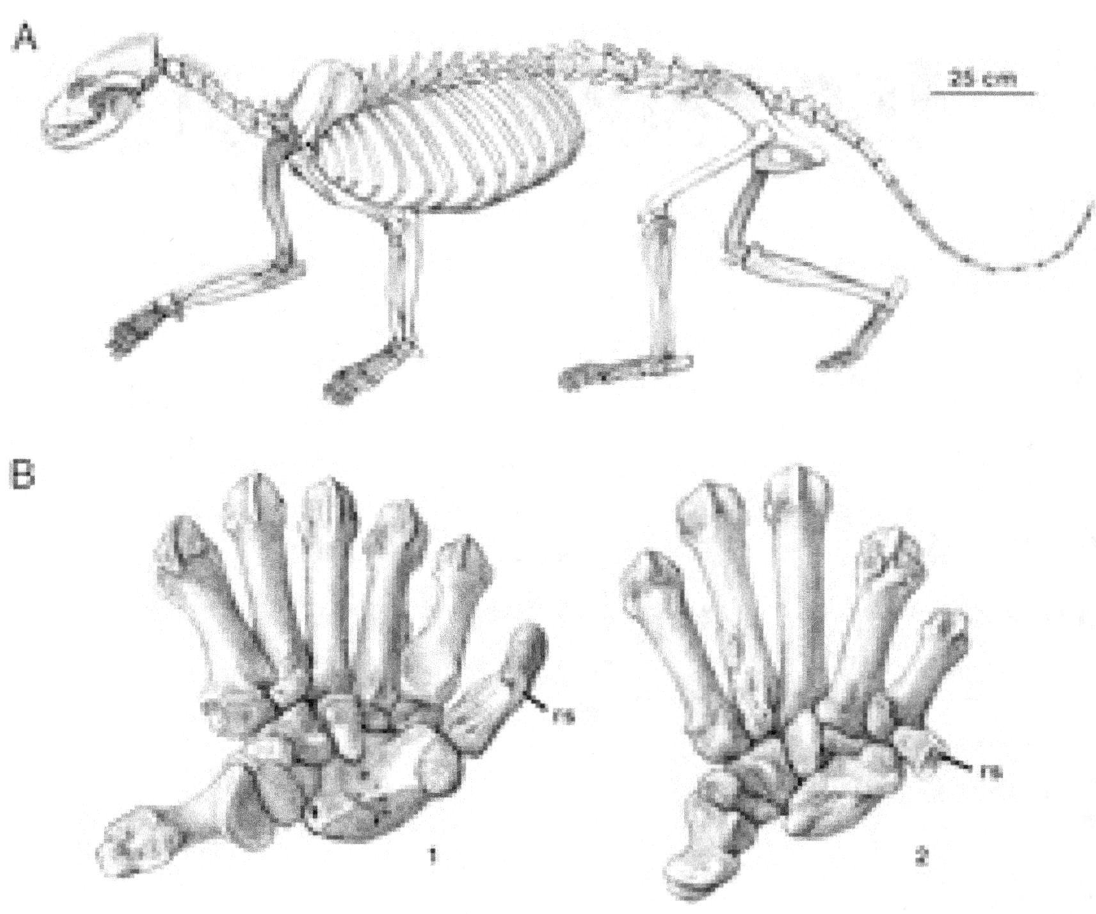

# The Panda Habitat

The pandas' natural habitat is found in the mountainous regions of China, where they inhabit dense bamboo forests. These lush forests are characterized by cool temperatures, high altitudes, and misty clouds, creating the perfect environment for pandas to thrive.

Pandas are highly adapted to their habitat, with their unique black and white coat providing excellent camouflage among the shadows and snowy patches of the forest. They are also skilled climbers, utilizing their strong forelimbs and sharp claws to navigate the steep terrain and tall bamboo trees.

Bamboo is the primary source of food for pandas, and their habitat must provide ample bamboo resources to sustain their diet. Pandas can consume up to 40 pounds (18 kg) of bamboo per day, and their habitat must have enough bamboo to support their dietary needs.

Unfortunately, the pandas' habitat is under threat due to human activities such as logging, agriculture, and infrastructure development.

Deforestation has resulted in habitat loss and fragmentation, isolating panda populations and reducing their access to food and suitable breeding grounds. Climate change is also affecting their habitat, with rising temperatures and changing rainfall patterns impacting bamboo growth.

Conservation efforts are underway to protect and restore panda habitat, including the creation of protected areas and reforestation initiatives. These efforts aim to safeguard the pandas' habitat and ensure that they have a suitable environment to thrive and continue to exist in the wild.

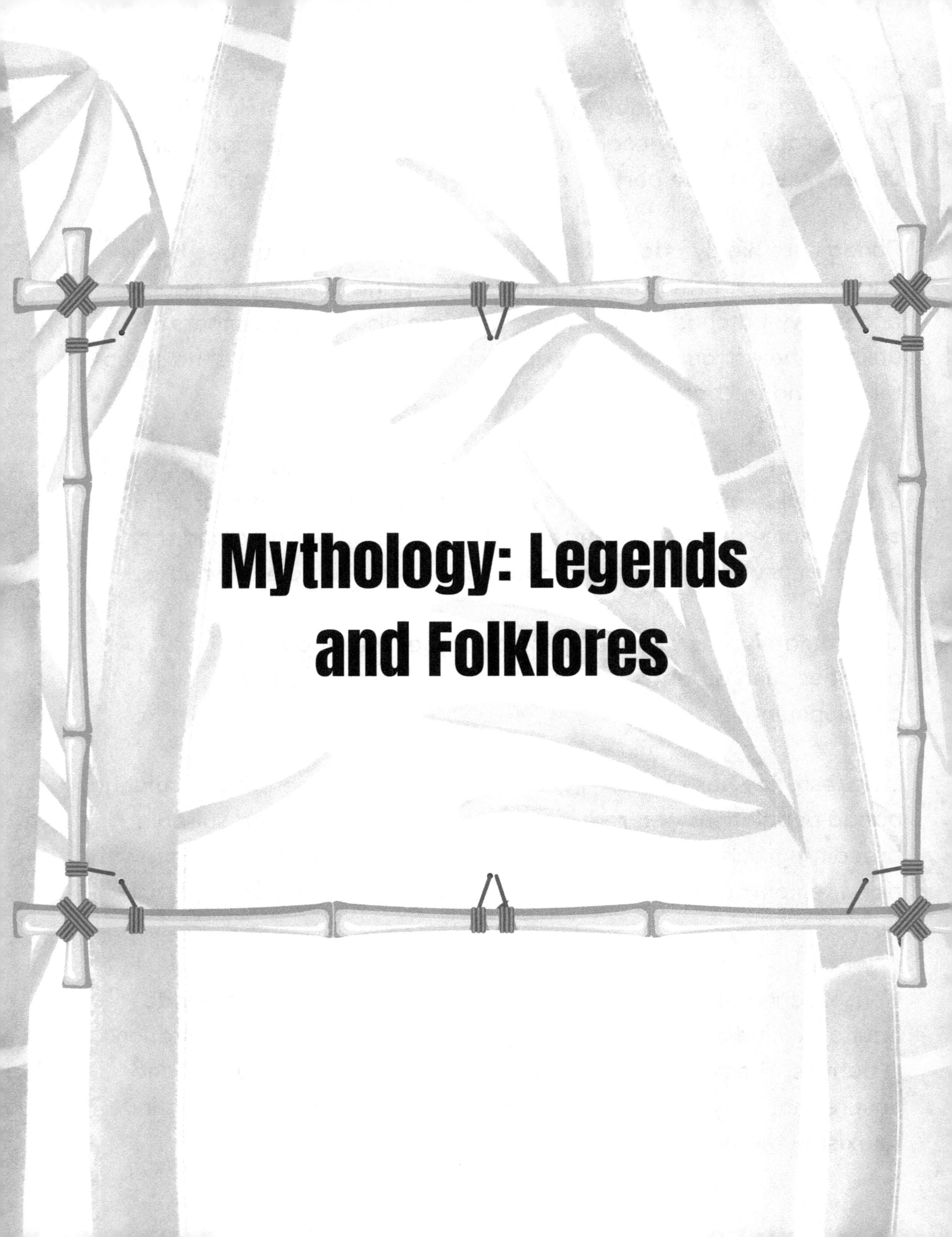

# Mythology: Legends and Folklores

Pandas have been revered in many cultures, and over the years, they have become the subjects of numerous legends and folktales. These stories have been passed down through generations, capturing the imagination of people around the world. Here are some fascinating myths and tales associated with pandas.

Pandas have also been featured in various folktales from other cultures, where they are often depicted as symbols of strength, resilience, and wisdom. These myths and legends highlight the cultural significance and mystique associated with pandas, adding to their allure as one of the most beloved and iconic animals on Earth.

From China to Tibet, Japan to other parts of the world, pandas have captured the hearts and minds of people through their legendary status in folklore and mythology. These stories have contributed to the cultural significance and reverence for pandas, making them more than just animals, but also symbols of hope, luck, and wisdom in many traditions.

Read on to see more about the various mythologies around pandas from Japan, China, and Tibet.

In Tibetan folklore, pandas are believed to be messengers of the gods and are revered as sacred animals. They are believed to have the ability to communicate with the divine world and are often seen as protectors of the forests and mountains.

In Chinese mythology, pandas are believed to possess magical powers and are often considered symbols of peace, harmony, and good luck. It is believed that pandas can ward off evil spirits and bring prosperity and happiness to those who encounter them. Pandas are also associated with the yin-yang symbol, representing the balance between opposing forces in the universe.

In Japanese folklore, pandas are believed to possess the ability to transform into humans and are often depicted as wise and powerful creatures. They are believed to bring blessings and good fortune to those who encounter them and are considered to be symbols of longevity and abundance.

# The Panda Diet:
# More Than Just Bamboo...
# and Bathroom Habits!

Pandas are famous for their love of bamboo, but did you know that their dietary habits extend beyond just munching on leaves? Pandas have some unique bathroom habits that are both intriguing and funny!

When it comes to peeing, pandas have a quirky habit of doing it while standing on their front paws, which is also known as a handstand! Yes, you read that right - pandas perform handstands while going pee! It's like a gymnastics routine in the wild!

But that's not all - pandas are also known or their frequent bathroom breaks. A panda can poop up to 40 times a day! That's a lot of potty breaks for these adorable bears! It's like having a never-ending supply of bamboo and a constant need for bathroom breaks.

Pandas have a unique digestive system that requires them to consume large amounts of bamboo to meet their nutritional needs. However, their bodies aren't efficient at extracting nutrients from bamboo, which results in a high frequency of bathroom trips. It's like a digestive marathon for these furry bamboo eaters!

Despite their peculiar bathroom habits, pandas are well-adapted to their bamboo diet. They have a strong jaw and sharp teeth for stripping bamboo leaves and bark, and a specialized wrist bone that acts like a thumb to help them grip the stalks. It's like a precision bamboo-eating machine with some hilarious bathroom quirks!

Unfortunately, deforestation reduces the availability of bamboo, the primary food source for pandas. As trees are cleared to make way for agriculture, logging, and infrastructure development, the panda's natural habitat is disrupted, leading to loss of foraging areas and decreased bamboo density. Additionally, climate change can further exacerbate the issue by making it harder for pandas to find sufficient food. These combined factors pose serious threats to the panda's survival, as they rely heavily on bamboo for their dietary needs and are highly specialized herbivores adapted to a specific habitat. Conservation efforts to protect the panda's habitat, promote reforestation, and mitigate the impacts of climate change are crucial for their long-term survival.

While pandas may be known for their love of bamboo, they also have some interesting and funny bathroom habits that make them truly unique and fascinating creatures in the animal kingdom.

# Panda Cubs: Adorable and Growing Up Fast

Panda babies, or cubs, are among the cutest creatures on Earth. Born blind and helpless, they rely entirely on their mother for care and protection. Panda cubs are usually born in a warm den, and they spend their first few months snuggled up with their mother, nursing and sleeping.

As they grow, panda cubs become more curious and adventurous. They start crawling, playing, and exploring their surroundings, but always staying close to their mother. Cubs learn important skills, such as climbing trees, from their mother's guidance.

Cubs have a voracious appetite and start eating bamboo around six months of age, but they continue nursing from their mother until they are about 18 months old. As they get older, cubs become more independent, and they start venturing out on their own to explore and learn valuable survival skills.

Panda cubs are born with a thick coat of white fur, but as they grow, their fur changes to the iconic black-and-white pattern that pandas are known for. They also develop their own unique personalities, with some cubs being more playful and outgoing, while others are more reserved and shy.

These cubs have a special place in the hearts of people around the world, and their playful antics and adorable looks have made them beloved animal ambassadors. They are a symbol of hope for the conservation of their species and a reminder of the importance of protecting their natural habitats so future generations to enjoy these precious creatures.

# Mama and Cubs

Threats to
Panda Survival:
A Call for Conservation

Pandas face numerous dangers that put their survival at risk. One of the biggest threats is habitat loss, as their natural bamboo forests are being destroyed to make way for agriculture, logging, and human development. This loss of habitat disrupts their food source and disrupts their ability to find shelter, leading to increased stress and reduced reproduction rates.

Another danger is climate change, which affects the availability of bamboo, their primary food source. Changes in temperature, rainfall patterns, and habitat quality can impact the growth and distribution of bamboo, affecting the pandas' ability to find enough food to sustain themselves.

Illegal poaching and hunting for their fur, as well as the capture of pandas for the illegal wildlife trade, also pose significant threats to their survival. Although poaching has declined in recent years, it still remains a concern for the long-term survival of panda populations.

In addition, the fragmentation of panda habitats due to human activities, such as roads and infrastructure development, disrupts their movement and leads to isolation of populations, reducing their genetic diversity and making them more vulnerable to diseases and other threats.

Conservation efforts, such as habitat protection, anti-poaching measures, and community engagement, are crucial in mitigating these threats and ensuring the survival of pandas in the wild.

# Hangin' Out

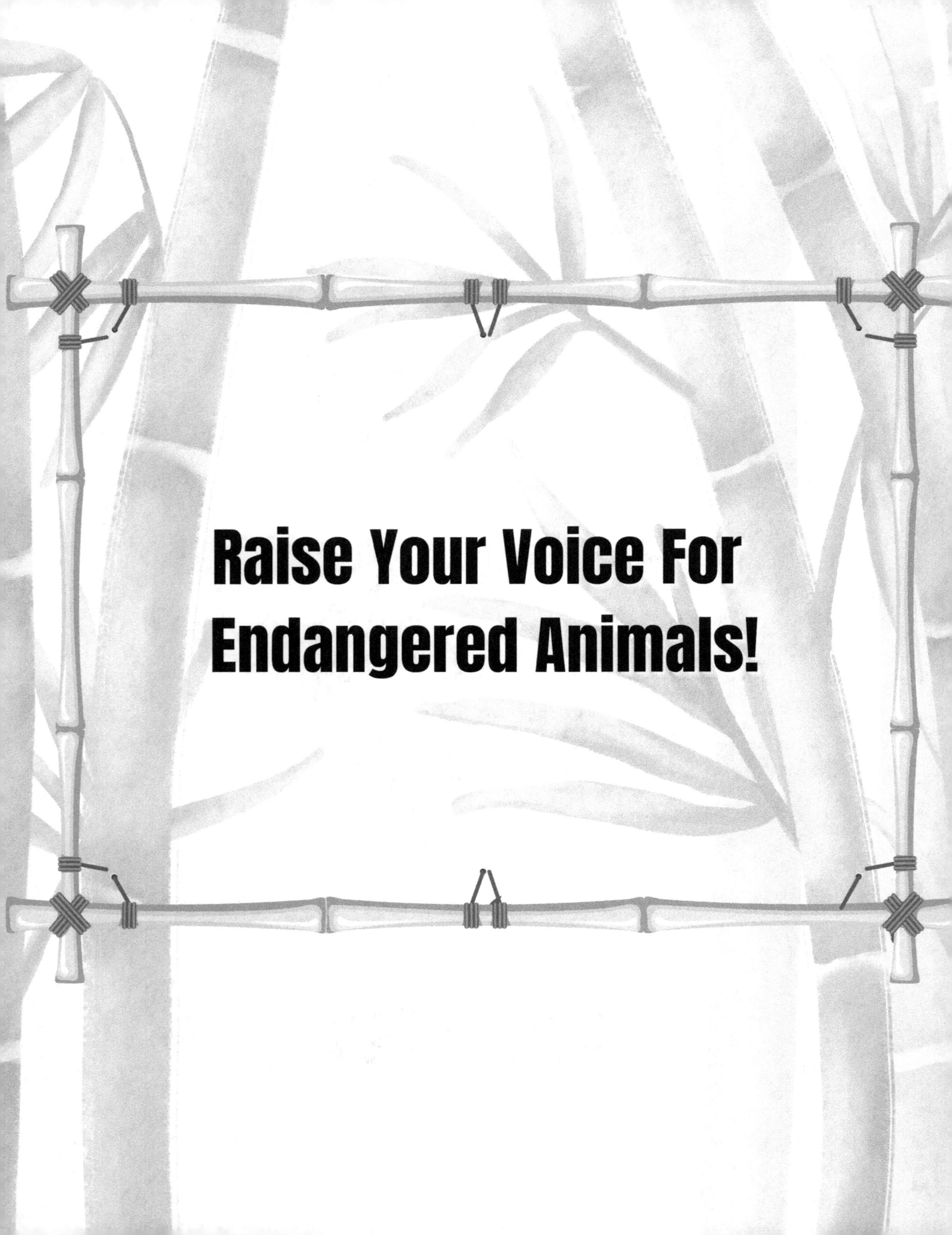

Raise Your Voice For
Endangered Animals!

The illegal wildlife trade is a multi-billion dollar industry, and pandas are among the most vulnerable animals on earth. Their unique appearance and cultural significance have made them highly sought after, leading to rampant poaching and trafficking. This has resulted in a drastic decline in panda populations, with some species on the brink of extinction.

But pandas are not the only vulnerable targets. Many other species are also at risk due to habitat destruction, climate change, and other human activities. It's up to all of us to take action to protect these animals and their habitats.

One way to get involved is to support reputable conservation organizations dedicated to panda conservation efforts.

By taking action to protect pandas and their habitats, we can ensure that these adorable animals will continue to thrive for generations to come. So let's join together and make a difference in safeguarding the future of pandas and their natural habitats.

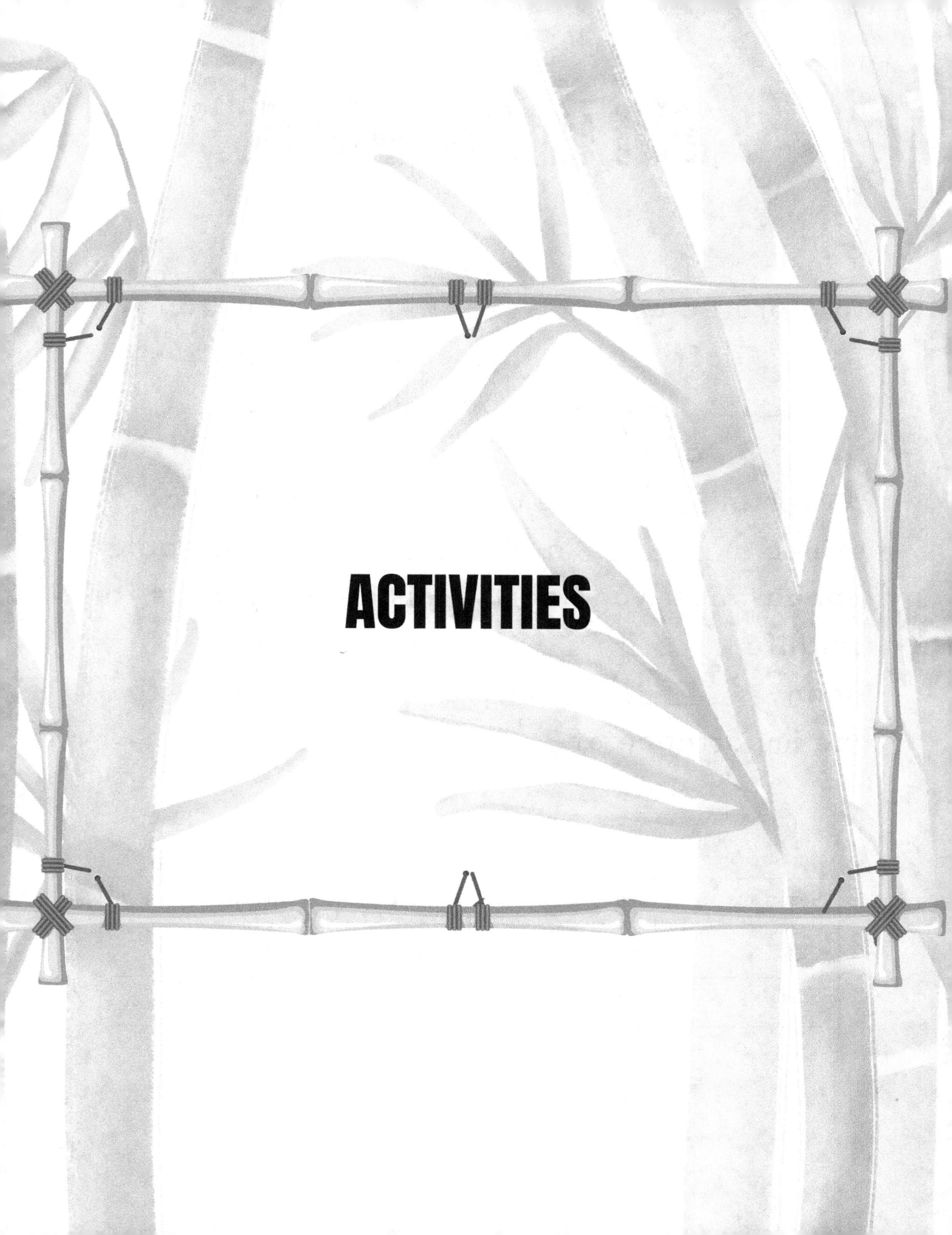
ACTIVITIES

# Fill in the Blank

In a protected ________, a giant, black and
______ fluffy _____ named Benny, an
__________ species, roamed among the
________ and __________ trees. With
powerful _____, he climbed with grace, a
skilled _________ and ________. His adorable
appearance won hearts, raising awareness for
wildlife __________ and biodiversity.
Benny's _________ thrived in a testament to
the importance of ________ efforts.

| forest | bear | endangered | herbivore |
| white | paws | protecting | eucalyptus |
| climber | bamboo | conservation | habitat |

# Fill in the Blank

## A N S W E R   K E Y

In a protected habitat, a giant, black and white fluffy bear named Benny, an endangered species, roamed among the bamboo and eucalyptus trees. With powerful paws, he climbed with grace, a skilled climber and herbivore. His adorable appearance won hearts, raising awareness for protecting wildlife and biodiversity. Benny's forest thrived in a testament to the importance of conservation efforts.

| forest | bear | endangered | herbivore |
| --- | --- | --- | --- |
| white | paws | protecting | eucalyptus |
| climber | bamboo | conservation | habitat |

# Help the panda reach the bamboo!

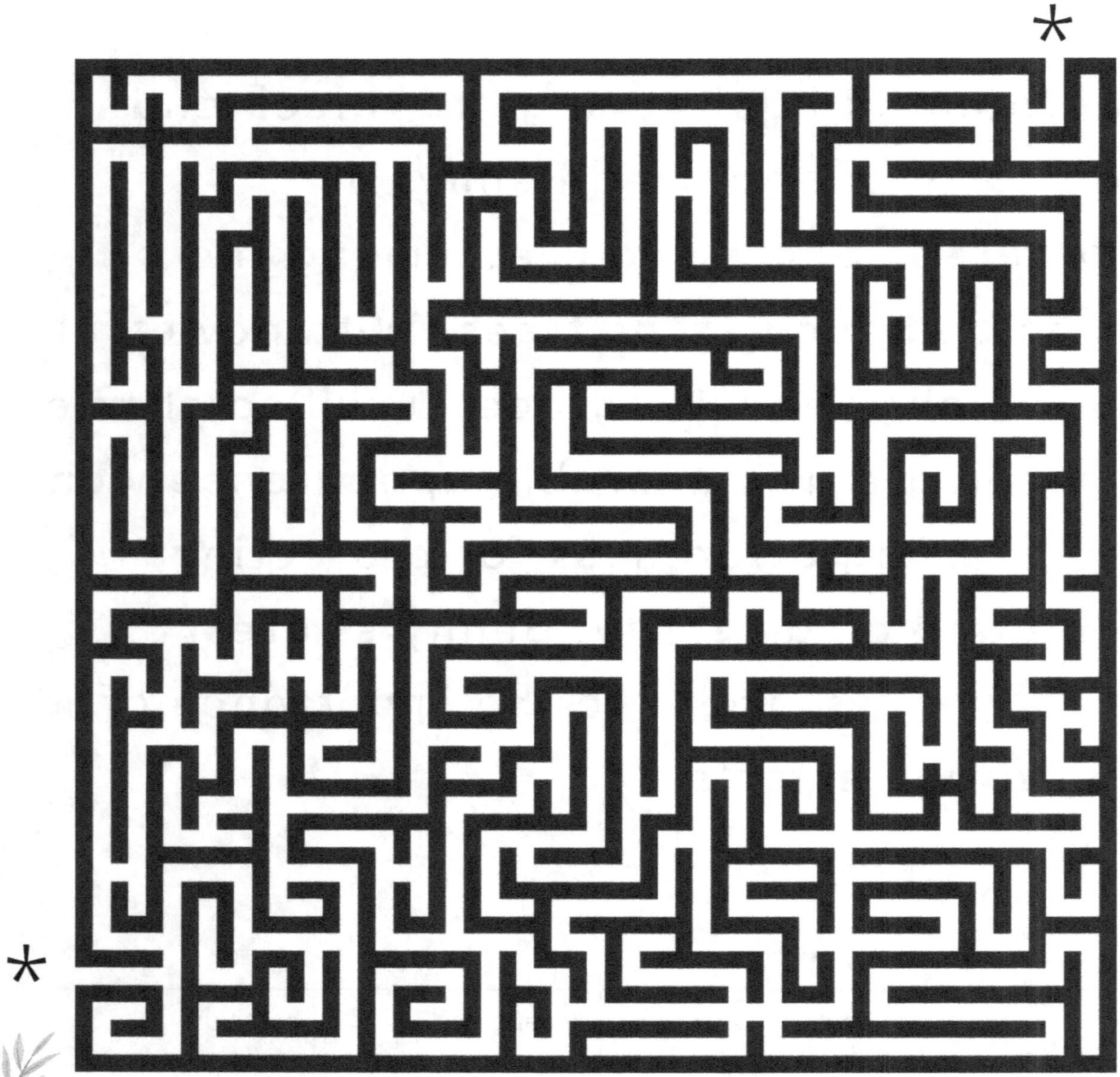

# Word Search

```
V E B Q J P A B V R Y J C Q H C A X F Q
Z Q N I H A B I T A T Y P W U O J Z M X
V J A D O R A B L E K L T W P N I X T L
W S R V A D I C P H Z L R C K S D P Q O
S F U N R N I H E Z A B E U E E F N G T
Q L U I U Q G V A K Q F E T X R C U C I
M A E N C W U E E L E T S E P V F A T Z
C X B U M C B N R R C Q U C R A O T Z S
N L B V C P R U K E S C E V A T R J J H
M S I A Z A R U C O D I Q T M I E J W P
T N J M M U L O P I G T T Y W O S R U A
F J P X B B Z Y T W T C W Y J N T C Q D
T G A V L E O S P E B Z U L M L M Z J D
N C W O A F R O D T C E W I L D L I F E
K Q S P C M L X K A U T A G S H G W P D
M V G A K V A U M B Y S E R H W H I T E
R I F Z O B K M F X T S S D N D R Y X Q
U U X U K F N Y M F H E R B I V O R E G
R V O X J Q B V M A Y P I P Y R M K A O
Y J G I A N T T X E L L J S V G Q G G W
```

| | | |
|---|---|---|
| conservation | biodiversity | endangered |
| protected | eucalyptus | herbivore |
| adorable | habitat | wildlife |
| climber | bamboo | mammal |
| fluffy | giant | forest |
| black | white | bear |
| cute | trees | paws |

39

# A N S W E R   K E Y

## Word Search

```
V E B Q J P A B V R Y J C Q H C A X F Q
Z Q N I H A B I T A T Y P W U O J Z M X
V J A D O R A B L E K L T W P N I X T L
W S R V A D I C P H Z L R C K S D P Q O
S F U N R N I H E Z A B E U E E F N G T
Q L U I U Q G V A K Q F E T X R C U C I
M A E N C W U E E L E T S E P V F A T Z
C X B U M C B N R R C Q U C R A O T Z S
N L B V C P R U K E S C E V A T R J J H
M S I A Z A R U C O D I Q T M I E J W P
T N J M M U L O P I G T T Y W O S R U A
F J P X B B Z Y T W T C W Y J N T C Q D
T G A V L E O S P E B Z U L M L M Z J D
N C W O A F R O D T C E W I L D L I F E
K Q S P C M L X K A U T A G S H G W P D
M V G A K V A U M B Y S E R H W H I T E
R I F Z O B K M F X T S S D N D R Y X Q
U U X U K F N Y M F H E R B I V O R E G
R V O X J Q B V M A Y P I P Y R M K A O
Y J G I A N T T X E L L J S V G Q G G W
```

| | | |
|---|---|---|
| conservation | biodiversity | endangered |
| protected | eucalyptus | herbivore |
| adorable | habitat | wildlife |
| climber | bamboo | mammal |
| fluffy | giant | forest |
| black | white | bear |
| cute | trees | paws |

# Panda-monium!

## Across

**4.** Land of Pandas

**6.** bright colored type

**9.** Po's home

**10.** Black and White Coloring

**13.** unusual bathroom pose

**14.** hilly home

## Down

**1.** Grassy chow

**2.** a kind that's little

**3.** balance and harmony

**5.** where the trees grow tall

**7.** depends on us

**8.** island nation with pandas

**11.** its a wrist!

**12.** Reedy food

# Panda-monium!

**ANSWER KEY**

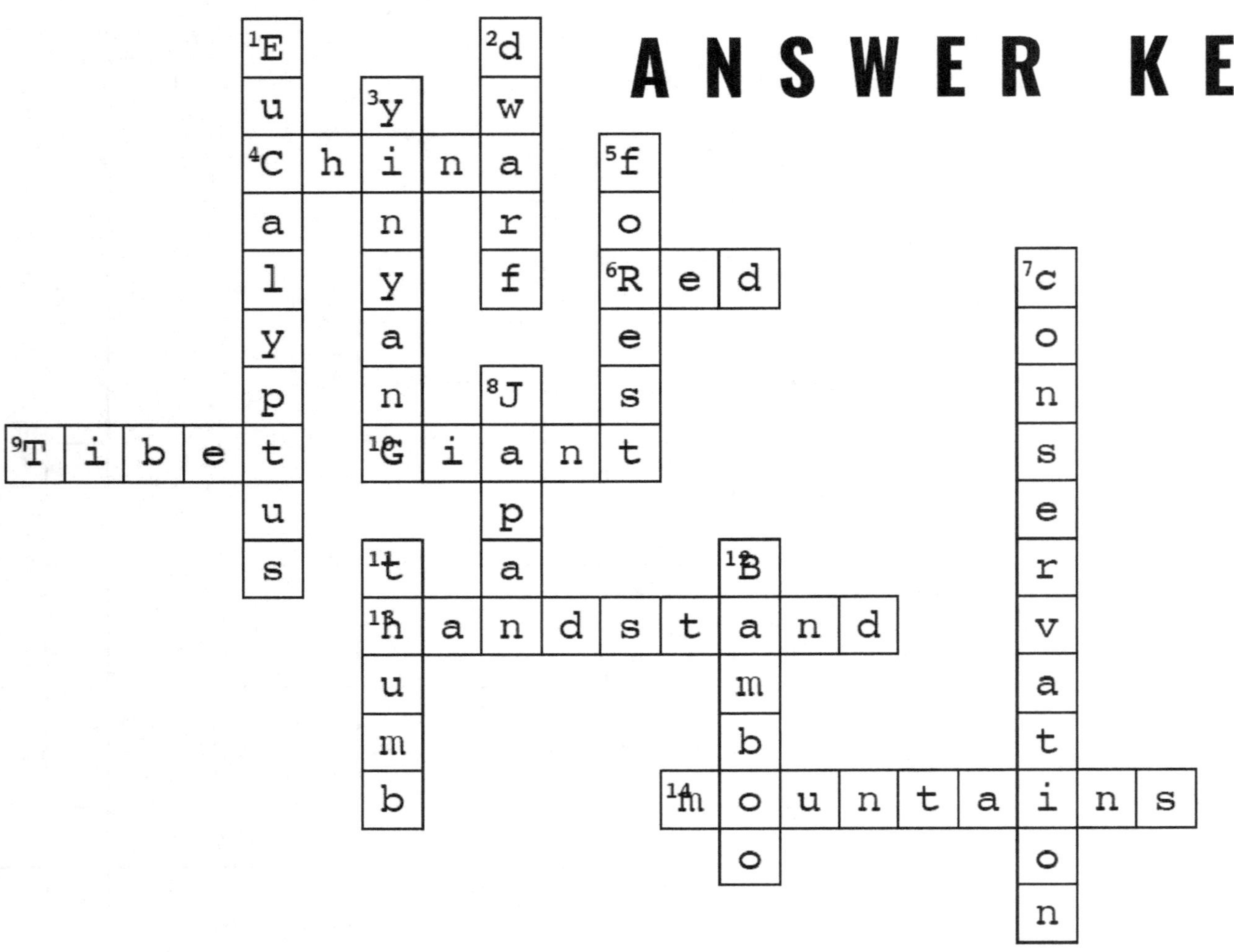

## Across

**4.** Land of Pandas

**6.** bright colored type

**9.** Po's home

**10.** Black and White Coloring

**13.** unusual bathroom pose

**14.** hilly home

## Down

**1.** Grassy chow

**2.** a kind that's little

**3.** balance and harmony

**5.** where the trees grow tall

**7.** depends on us

**8.** island nation with pandas

**11.** its a wrist!

**12.** Reedy food

42

# Panda Pop Quiz!

Were you paying attention? See if you can answer the following questions.

**1** What are the main threats to pandas in the wild?

_______________________________________________

_______________________________________________

**2** How much do adult pandas weigh on average?

_______________________________________________

_______________________________________________

**3** What is the average lifespan of a wild panda?

_______________________________________________

_______________________________________________

**4** How many hours a day do pandas spend eating bamboo?

_______________________________________________

_______________________________________________

**5** Where do pandas live in the wild?

_______________________________________________

_______________________________________________

**6** Can a panda do a handstand?

_______________________________________________

_______________________________________________

# ANSWER KEY
## Panda Pop Quiz!

Were you paying attention? See if you can answer the following questions.

**1** What are the main threats to pandas in the wild?

**The main threats to pandas in the wild are habitat loss due to deforestation, climate change affecting their food supply, and illegal hunting and poaching.**

**2** How much do adult pandas weigh on average?

**Adult pandas weigh on average about 200 to 300 pounds.**

**3** What is the average lifespan of a wild panda?

**The average lifespan of a wild panda is around 15 to 20 years.**

**4** How many hours a day do pandas spend eating bamboo?

**Pandas spend around 10 to 16 hours a day eating bamboo to meet their dietary needs.**

**5** Where do pandas live in the wild?

**Pandas live in the wild in the mountainous regions of China, primarily in the Sichuan, Shaanxi, and Gansu provinces.**

**6** Can a panda do a handstand?

**No, pandas cannot do handstands as they are not physically built for such activities, however, they do stand on their hands to wee up a tree sometimes!**

THANKS
for reading

www.ingramcontent.com/pod-product-compliance
Lightning Source LLC
Chambersburg PA
CBHW081542250726
48659CB00009B/3043